Promptings
from
Paradise

J. Philip Newell

Paulist Press
New York/Mahwah, N.J.

Cover design by Cindy Dunne

Book design by Lynn Else

First published in Great Britain in 1998
by Triangle/SPCK, Holy Trinity Church, Marylebone Road,
London NW1 4DU.

Library of Congress Cataloging-in-Publication Data

Newell, J. Philip.
Promptings from paradise / J. Philip Newell.
p.   cm.
ISBN 0-8091-3935-9 (alk. paper)
1. Spiritual life—Christianity. 2. Bible. N.T. Gospels—Devotional use. I. Title.
BV4501.2.N534 2000
248.4´82—dc21
99-088940

Published by Paulist Press
997 Macarthur Boulevard
Mahwah, New Jersey 07430

www.paulistpress.com

Printed and bound in the
United States of America

Contents

To my youngest child,
Cameron John Philip Magnus,
who still conveys to me
the innocence of paradise.

Foreword

Shortly after Easter, 1997, I asked Philip Newell to prepare a course for use in the parishes of the Portsmouth Diocese, based on a vision of the nature of the Christian mission that was breaking through to us. Visions and mission statements are two for a penny these days, but we still felt drawn to some kind of basic description of who and what we were supposed to be—namely, a church that prays to its Lord, that engages with the world, and that hears and proclaims the good news. A church, after all, that did not base its whole being on worship, that was uninterested in the confusions and challenges of the world, and that was unready to do anything to the gospel except package it, would be a fairly dull and uninspiring community!

Philip duly produced a course that many of us used in 1998, and to which, I suspect, many of us will keep returning in the years ahead. You will find here a narrative of Christianity that is neither slick nor easy; more to the point, it keeps drawing us, through biblical and acute observation on human nature, again and again back to God, to the world, and to ourselves. Those who want a worthy and self-conscious Christianity that measures success in the world's terms are wasting their time if they read any further. But for those who are ready and willing to see God ahead of them, in whatever experiences may befall them, this messy—and deeply biblical and Catholic—vision of Christian discipleship will be both stimulating and nourishing.

KENNETH STEVENSON
The Bishop of Portsmouth

Preface

Jesus said, "The kingdom of God is within you" (Lk 17:21). An equivalent early British image of "kingdom of God" is "paradise of God." The paradise or garden of God is within us. Although we may have lost sight of its beauty, or cut ourselves off from it, it is at the beginning and heart of all that has been created. From God's life, our life and all life has arisen. What does it mean, therefore, to live in relationship to the mystery of God? Part of what is meant relates to the very ground of our being and world. That is where we are to look, for that is the place of God's hidden dwelling. As St. John the Divine writes in his revelation of love, "the home of God is among mortals" (Rv 19:3). Although we may live in exile from that heart of life, promptings can still be heard from deep within us and among us.

In *One Foot in Eden* I wrote of the root that connects us still to the goodness of the garden in which we and all things have our origin. We bear within ourselves the image of God. Yes, that image may be covered over by all sorts of confusions and wrongdoings in our lives and world (sometimes to such an extent that we cease to believe it is there), but it is the essence of who we are. How is that image to be recovered at the different stages of life's journey? Only through the gift of grace. But let us remember that both grace and nature are gifts of God. Our natural being is a gift from God that comes to us through creation. Our well-being is also a gift from God. It is a grace that restores us to our true selves, freeing us from the falseness that overlays the essential goodness of our natural being. The gift of redemption, then, is given to release in us what has been most deeply and naturally planted by God. The Creator and the Redeemer are one.

This book is an attempt to explore what that means in relation to our understanding and practice of prayer, and in relation to our expectations of where the Word of God is to be heard. It is also an attempt to underline the connection between a practice of prayer and contemplation on the one hand and a passionate engagement in the life of the world on the other. My primary hope for this book, however, is not merely that we may have more thoughts about these matters. Rather it is that we may experience God addressing us in the depths of our being, renewing us and challenging us. At the end of each chapter there is a contemplative exercise, designed to help us listen at levels deep within ourselves.

The method of gospel contemplation that is used in this book grows out of what is called the Ignatian tradition. St. Ignatius of Loyola (1495–1556), founder of the religious community called the Society of Jesus (or the Jesuits), developed a simple but rich way of meditating and praying in relation to gospel stories. For centuries it was the preserve primarily of monastic communities and of those with life-vocations to prayer and contemplation. Now, however, it is being used by many others—particularly by lay people—in the realization that at one level we are all contemplatives. An important key to the method's use is to regard the imagination as a gift from God. It is given, as in the case of a child's imagination, or an artist's or scientist's, to lead us further into truth, not *away* from it. Through the use of the imagination, in which our stories, or our lives, are woven into Jesus' story, we can allow ourselves to be personally addressed by the Spirit of God at work within our spirits. Because this book was written largely during the year of St. Luke in the Revised Common Lectionary cycle, the great bulk of scripture references and quotations are from the Gospel according to St. Luke.

While the gospel contemplation exercises are designed for individual use, it can be extremely helpful to experience them in a group context. Often it is in sharing with others that we grasp most clearly what we have experienced within ourselves during a time of silent contemplation. The appendix, which offers guidance for group usage, is included for such adaptation.

Preface

This book in fact grew out of the shared contemplations of a group of women and men from throughout the Diocese of Portsmouth. My thanks go especially to them for their time and inspiration, as well as to Kenneth, my Bishop, for his vision and kind encouragements.

J. PHILIP NEWELL
St. John's House

1

Promptings in the World

In that region there were shepherds living in the fields, keeping watch over their flock by night. Then an angel of the Lord stood before them, and the glory of the Lord shone around them, and they were terrified. But the angel said to them, "Do not be afraid; for see—I am bringing you good news of great joy for all the people: to you is born this day in the city of David a Savior, who is the Christ, the Lord. This will be a sign for you: you will find a child wrapped in bands of cloth and lying in a manger." And suddenly there was with the angel a multitude of the heavenly host, praising God and saying, "Glory to God in the highest heaven, and on earth peace, good will among people." When the angel had left them and gone into heaven, the shepherds said to one another, "Let us go now to Bethlehem and see this thing that has taken place, which the Lord has made known to us." So they went with haste and found Mary and Joseph, and the child lying in the manger. When they saw this, they made known what had been told them about this child; and all who heard it were amazed at what the shepherds told them. But Mary treasured all these words and pondered them in her heart. (Lk 2:8-20)

I t is stating the obvious to say that Jesus was not born in a church. In fact, it is *so* obvious that we can miss the point! Jesus, the Savior of the world, was born in a stable in Bethlehem. His birth, life, death and resurrection were utterances of God, spoken and first heard in the world. Only then was this mystery proclaimed in synagogues and churches.

The same can be said, as St. John does, of "the Word" that was in the beginning. "All things," he says, "came into being through him, and without him not one thing came into being" (Jn 1:3). That is to say that all life has been uttered into being. As the ninth-century Irish teacher Eriugena said, "If God were to stop speaking, all things would cease to exist." Life in its essence is an expression of God. The place of God's speaking, therefore, is the world. That is where we are to listen. At the heart of all life, at the heart of our own lives, the mystery of God is being unfolded.

But we are not to draw a hard and fast distinction between the world and the church. The church is part of the world. Hearing in the world and hearing in the church are like listening in stereo. The tendency in religion, however, is to so cherish our own tradition of hearing that we begin to act as if God can only be heard in and through us. "Ever since the creation of the world," as St. Paul says, "his eternal power and divine nature, invisible though they are, have been understood and seen through the things that are made" (Rom 1:20).

A favorite theme in St. Luke's Gospel is to interweave the "holy" people with *all* people, or the church with the world. In the story of the presentation of the Christ child in the temple, St. Luke records the wise old Simeon speaking of a salvation that has been "prepared in the presence of all peoples" (Lk 2:31). Similarly, Luke sets John the Baptist's proclaiming of the Word in the context of what is happening both religiously and politically. "In the fifteenth year of the reign of Emperor Tiberius," he says, "when Pontius Pilate was governor of Judea, and...during the high priesthood of Annas and Caiaphas, the word of God came to John son of Zechariah in the wilderness" (Lk 3:1-2). The Word is uttered not in a religious vacuum but in the context of the whole of life. It is spoken in relation to all people and to all things, whether that be the high priest and religion, the governor and politics, or the emperor and the whole of the known world.

Jesus speaks of men and women beyond his own religious tradition who hear the Word of God and faithfully respond to it (Lk 4:25ff). The Queen of the South and the people of Nineveh have heard it, he says, and yet the ears of his own people are closed (Lk 11:29ff). Similarly, in one of his greatest parables, that of the Good Samaritan, Jesus describes the falseness of a priest and a Levite while praising the truthfulness of a man from Samaria, a nation racially despised by the "holy" people of Israel because of their pagan inheritance (Lk 10:29ff). The extent to which Jesus points well beyond the bounds of religion to examples of faithfulness is highlighted in the story of the Roman centurion who believes that his slave will be made well simply by Jesus uttering a word of healing. "Not even in Israel," says Jesus, "have I found such faith" (Lk 7:9).

In our gospel passage the shepherds represent this in the extreme. They are "sinners," uneducated in religious teaching and practice. They are on the fringes of society, mistrusted by townsfolk as lawless outsiders, "living in the fields" as St. Luke says. Yet they hear the "good news" of the Christ child's birth and announce it. As Jesus says later in St. Luke's

Gospel, there are all sorts of people, from east and west and from north and south, who unexpectedly "will eat in the kingdom of God" (Lk 13:29). They are the ones, rather than those who now religiously exalt themselves, who "will be first." They, like the prophets, have heard in their lives the intimations of God and they bear witness to what they have heard.

What is it in us that hesitates to let the shepherds in, as it were, or to receive from them an announcement of God for our lives? Why is it that there is so little expectation in our traditions that the truth will be spoken from beyond the bounds of conventional religion? Even in relation to ourselves we are often loath to hear the promptings of God arise from wild or uneducated dimensions of who we are. In part it is because the language and style of the "shepherd" are so different from normal religious expression. Do we assume that the Mystery is expressed in only one tongue? Let us never lose sight of the multiplicity of utterances by God in the life-forms of earth, sea and sky, and in the varied races and people of the earth. They are all at heart expressions of God, even though we may not yet have learned how to listen to them.

Not only was the perfect utterance of God, namely Jesus, delivered in a stable and not in a church; it was a birthplace of no respectability whatever. We need not be romantic about the manger setting. Its equivalent today would be the garage behind the local pub. It had neither the familiarity of a home nor the safety of a hospital. Such a birth was filled with risk, and there was no one there of any respected authority to testify to it and declare it to be "holy." But is that not the way of God, as witnessed to again and again in the scriptures, the One who speaks in burning bushes and dreams, and in the earth's oppressed and neglected people?

There tends to be fear, and perhaps rightly so, about hearing the Word in the world. It is not always a safe place, and its boundaries are not well defined. Who knows what we will hear and be called to do? As Jesus says of the Spirit, "It blows where it chooses, and you hear the sound of it, but you do not know where it comes from or where it goes" (Jn 3:8). Listening for the promptings of God in the world may open us to new and strange perspectives. No wonder we are fearful. We are listening to the indefinable and awesome mystery of God. Rather than suppress these fears, we need to rediscover their rightful place in the church if we are to avoid religion's tendency to domesticate the Word.

It was on a mountain covered in cloud that a special revelation of Christ was given in the words, "This is my Son, my Beloved; listen to him" (Lk 9:35). The cloud is a symbol of the unknowable. The disciples were being guided further into a knowledge of Christ, but not in a way that reduced him to neat and tame definitions. God is beyond knowledge, and while in Christ we come to know that love is at the heart of the Mystery, the cloud is always the context of our knowing. We may well be fearful of the unknowable. At the same time, however, an assurance is given for both our listening in the church and in the world. To the shepherds in the fields, as to Zechariah in the temple, the message is, "Do not be afraid" (Lk 1:13; 2:10). Know that what is being uttered is "good news" (Lk 1:19; 2:10). Though it may be surrounded by confusions and uncertainties, it is a word of "great joy for all the people" (Lk 2:10).

Where in particular ought we to be listening for the promptings of God? No limitations are to be set, for the world is God's dwelling place. It may be in the intuitions of a poet or in the cries of an oppressed people. It may be in the tears of a mother weeping over the loss of her child or in the light of the morning sun rising over the waters. It can be heard issuing up out of the heart of life, from both its joy and its sorrow. It is spoken not from afar but from the center of all things.

After Jesus' death two of his followers hear the truth in the mouth of "a stranger." While they are slow to recognize their Savior, they later say, "Were not our hearts burning within us while he was talking to us on the road?" (Lk 24:32). It is in the breaking of bread at an ordinary village table that their eyes are finally opened to the presence of Christ. So in our lives, by the inner sight of faith, it is in the midst of the daily sharing of food, as well as in the breaking apart of life when pain and struggle open new doors of perception in us, that we can be alert to the presence of God. Part of being alert is noticing when our hearts are "burning within us," for it is at the deepest of levels that the Mystery addresses us.

We have all experienced being stirred by the words and presence of another, or by others' joys and sufferings, even from afar. At the time of the death of the Princess of Wales there was an extraordinary depth of response in men and women throughout the world. What was happening? At one level it was a straightforward mourning and sense of loss. She left behind her two children. Countless others felt bereaved. At a deeper level, however, something else was occurring. Diana had reflected both physically and spiritually something of the beauty of life. In both her living and dying it was a beauty streaked through with pain and struggle. Which one of us does not know this to be true of life? We have seen it in our children and in creation. Life is essentially a gift of beauty. At times of loss and suffering, however, we know it to be wrapped in pain. Sometimes it is precisely in the midst of the brokenness of life that we become most sharply aware of its beauty. Did Diana's death not stir in us this type of awareness of the beauty and pain that are within each one of us?

Christ is the perfect image of the beauty that is at the beginning and center of all things. It is a beauty that was most powerfully revealed to us on the cross in the midst of his brokenness. There he prayed for those who were crucifying him, "Father, forgive them; for they do not know what they are doing" (Lk 23:34). These words lead us to the love that is at the heart of God, and thus at the heart of life. But is this the only place of suffering that we are to look to for a revelation of the mystery of God? Does it not rather guide us to be listening for the promptings of God wherever there is pain, and in the brokenness as well as the beauty of our own lives? Although the intimations of God may not always be clear to us, and may at times come through unexpected sources and painful moments, God's utterances will resonate with our deepest and most certain experiences of life and love. These are the things that we are to ponder, as Luke says, in our listening for God.

Gospel Contemplation

1   Prepare for the gospel contemplation by being still for a few minutes. Be aware of God's presence within and all around you.

2   Read and reread the gospel passage (Lk 2:8-20), letting its details settle in your memory.

3   Imagine the fields in which the shepherds live and the barn in which the Christ child is lying. What are they like? Spend at least five minutes using the senses of your imagination to see, hear, smell, taste and touch these places. Allow them to be a combination of places that you have known in your life.

4   What is your heart's desire? In your imagination envision Mary beside the manger looking you in the face and asking, "What is it you seek? What do you want?"

5   For at least ten minutes go back over the whole of the gospel passage, allowing the story to unfold further in your imagination. Who is there? What is being said? What is being done?

6   Gather together the main strands of your contemplation. Spend a few minutes giving attention to the parts of the contemplation that most deeply moved you. Conclude by saying the Lord's Prayer.

2

Promptings of the Church

When Jesus came to Nazareth, where he had been brought up, he went to the synagogue on the sabbath day, as was his custom. He stood up to read, and the scroll of the prophet Isaiah was given to him. He unrolled the scroll and found the place where it was written: "The Spirit of the Lord is upon me, because he has anointed me to bring good news to the poor. He has sent me to proclaim release to the captives and recovery of sight to the blind, to let the oppressed go free, to proclaim the year of the Lord's favor." And he rolled up the scroll, gave it back to the attendant, and sat down. The eyes of all in the synagogue were fixed on him. Then he began to say to them, "Today this scripture has been fulfilled in your hearing." (Lk 4:16-21)

earing the Word in the church and hearing the Word in the world are not opposed to each other. In fact, it is essential that we hold these two ways of listening together, for they are complementary parts of a whole. If torn apart, our hearing becomes prone to distortion. On the one hand, we begin to think that the Word can be heard only in the church, apart from the world. We begin to see those outside our religious tradition as having nothing to teach us. On the other hand, we can hear so broadly that we lose a distinctiveness of hearing, and miss the depth and precision of what has been heard in the church. We begin to attribute to God only vague notions of goodness and perfection, and miss the sharpness of Christ's revelation of God as passionate and suffering.

Jesus' practice of listening, as we have seen, was to hear from within religious tradition as well as from beyond it. This is a way of hearing that is alert to the utterance of God in all things. Jesus was forever breaking down the division between the "holy" people and "holy" place on the one hand, and all people and the whole of life on the other. St. Luke powerfully portrays this aspect of the gospel when, as Jesus breathes his last, the veil in the temple is torn in two (Lk 23:45). The inner sanctuary of the temple, known as the holy of holies, had been screened off by a veil, declaring the holy to be separate from the ordinary, and God to be distant from the realm of daily life. St. Luke depicts Jesus demonstrating the falseness of this separation. In him the holy is seen to interpenetrate the ordinary, and the ineffable mystery of God to be everywhere present. "The sanctuary of the Lord," as St. Luke calls the inner sanctum of the temple (Lk 1:9), can equally refer to God's dwelling place at the heart of all life.

To speak of finding God in all things is not to suggest that holy sites for prayer and pilgrimage and set times for meditation and worship are not important. But our sacred times and places for listening to the promptings of God need to be in tension with the practice of listening for God in the whole of life. We have known what it is to be moved by the words and sounds and scents of a holy place. My memory of hearing plainchant in the French Benedictine abbey of Saint-Wandrille, amid clouds of incense and an awareness that prayer had been offered up in this place for over a thousand years, is one such experience. But these moments need to be rooted in the much deeper mystery of God's Spirit brooding over the waters of all life (Gn 1:2), and of the intuitive response to that Mystery in the hearts of men and women when they are stirred to wonder, whether that be in looking into the face of a newborn child or in gazing across an open expanse of sea.

Not only is hearing in the church to bear a relationship to hearing in the world, the former needs actually to be guided by the latter. The mystery of God was being communicated in the world, through creation and in the lives of men and women, long before religion came into being. In fact it was the hearing of God in the world that gave rise to religion. In the Christian tradition we may claim a two-thousand-year tradition of hearing God in the church's mysteries of word and sacrament. It needs always, however, to be set in the context of the fifteen-billion-year tradition of God speaking in creation.

Part of what this perspective deepens in us is the realization that the Word is *not* ours. We do not possess it. It may be given particular expression through the church, but let us constantly remember that through the Word all things have come into being (Jn 1:1,3). Not only does the Word not belong to us, our relationship to it is to be that of "servants" (Lk 1:2). Like those who were "eyewitnesses" to Christ, says St. Luke, and faithfully conveyed what they had seen, so we are to serve the gospel. In proclaiming it we are not to assume that the Word is absent from the world. Part of our proclaiming is to affirm the people and places where the promptings of God are already being expressed in faithful relationship and creative action. And in preaching the "good news" we are not calling the world to become like us, but to become truly itself, for at heart the world is an utterance of God.

Our understanding of what it means to preach the good news needs constantly to be reexamined, if we are to avoid turning the Word into something either of our own possessing or of our own making. But this is not to question the imperative of sharing the truth that we have heard. Jesus describes himself as coming for this very reason (Lk 4:42), and he sends out the twelve with a similar purpose (Lk 9:2). Our vocation to share the good news is essential to our very being as the church.

It was Jesus' "custom," says St. Luke, to go to the synagogue on the sabbath day. This was a feature of his life and it played a part in what he proclaimed. He had not "heard" in a vacuum but from within the life of a community that was centuries old. His religious tradition, however, did not limit his hearing. This was his home, and the familiarity of its rituals and times and furnishings was part of his hearing. St. Luke, by referring to Nazareth and its synagogue as the place where he had been brought up, paints a picture of the context in which Jesus and his family before him for generations had been listening for the promptings of God. It was a tradition that believed that God had spoken "through the mouth of his holy prophets from of old," as Zechariah said (Lk 1:70). This was a wisdom passed down through a line of descent. It is a continuity of which the church has always seen itself as part, a tradition that can be enriched with time, with the wisdom of one generation being added to by another.

To say that the Word has been spoken to us through those who have gone before is not to suggest that it can be reduced to some external deposit of truth handed down from one generation to the next. The Word is a living utterance spoken by God from the heart of life at levels deeper than speech and thought. Although it may be received in and through the words of others, it cannot be captured in outward form. It is "living and active," says the writer to the Hebrews, "sharper than any two-edged sword" (Heb 4:12). It can pierce to the marrow of our souls, cutting through all sorts of falseness in us. It is this that we respond to in the writings of the prophets of old, when their words give expression to the promptings of God deep within us. *Their* words evoke what *we* know at one level but either have refused to pay heed to or been unable to grasp. At such moments our experience is not so much that of hearing the words of a prophet from the past as of being addressed by the Word of Life now. Our souls resonate with what we hear. Just as Elizabeth's child leapt in her womb when she heard Mary's words of greeting (Lk 1:41), so we can know within ourselves when we have heard the promptings of God in the utterances of another. They stir a passion in us or open a new awareness in our souls. Whether they be words of comfort or of challenge we know when our hearts have been thus addressed.

Words from the past have been preserved and cherished by the church because they give voice to our deepest experiences. Especially in the church's tradition of holy scripture, the writings of the great prophets and teachers are handed down to help us interpret the stirrings of God's Spirit in our own depths. In the words and sacraments of the church our inner hearing is drawn towards a conscious understanding. Sometimes the unarticulated hopes and fears that are in us are expressed in the prayers and hymns of those who have gone before. We bring our own limited experience as individuals to the church's centuries-old experience and find that we are given a language to express the mysteries of life and resurrection that stir within us.

We believe that Christ is the perfect expression of God. Part of that expression is a prophetic call for justice. The proclaiming of the gospel in the New Testament is introduced with the inclusion of one of the most unsettling prophetic characters, John the Baptist, wild and unkempt, living in the desert on a diet of locusts and honey, and calling on the world to change. To those who seek him out, his demanding words are, "Whoever has two coats must share with anyone who has none; and whoever has food must do likewise" (Lk 3:11). Similarly, the church has preserved the harsh and challenging words of Jesus, as well as his comforting ones. "How hard it is for those who have wealth," says Jesus, "to enter the kingdom of God" (Lk 18:24).

Such truths are easily forgotten in the world. Jesus spoke, for instance, of the need "to proclaim the year of the Lord's favor." These words refer to the Old Testament tradition of people being released from debt in the jubilee year (Lv 25). There is little hope of the crippling debt of the developing nations being lifted if the church does not play its part in witnessing to the urgent need for such liberation.

The fact that at times justice has been equally neglected in the church only makes the inclusion of such teachings in the gospel the more remarkable. Listening for the promptings of God from within the church will again and again bring us up against the costly demands of Jesus, and his insistence on self-giving (Lk 9:23ff). If when we gather as the church we come with an inner openness, then we will experience what it means for the Word to pierce our hearts. If when we gather we confess that we too are captives, and we too are blind, then the Book of Life will stay open for us and we will be a liberated people, increasingly restored in our inner sight.

When neglected truths are rediscovered in the church, there is always tension as to what the response will be. In the Old Testament account of the kings there is the story of a hidden book uncovered in the temple during the reign of King Josiah (2 Kgs 22). Josiah had ordered a renewing of the holy place, and it is in the beginnings of that renewal, as the treasury is being emptied out, that the book is rediscovered. In it is guidance for how the nation's life is to be ordered. The story provides an image of how truths, even at the heart of our tradition, can be lost. There is the need constantly to rediscover what has been known before. The Word may not be far from us, but often it is covered over, sometimes in the very place where we gather to hear.

Jesus was part of such an attempt to recover truth in his hometown synagogue. What he was uncovering was the Word of good news to the poor. His attempt was rejected. This was not because the people of Nazareth denied that such a message was part of their tradition, but rather because of Jesus' insistence that the promise was being fulfilled despite them, not because of them. They may have had words of liberation but the Word of liberation was being experienced elsewhere, in the lives of women and men open to its fulfilment. The gospel is given not primarily for intellectual or doctrinal assent but for the embodiment of truth in our lives. At its very inception Mary's receptive response had provided the model. To Gabriel, the messenger of promise, she says, "Let it be with me according to your word" (Lk 1:38).

Gospel Contemplation

1   Prepare for the gospel contemplation by being still for a few minutes. Be aware of God's presence within and all around you.

2   Read and reread the gospel passage (Lk 4:16–21), letting its details settle in your memory.

3   Imagine the synagogue in which Jesus is speaking. What is it like? Spend at least five minutes using the senses of your imagination to see, hear, smell, taste and touch the place. Allow it to be a combination of places that you have known in your life.

4   What is your heart's desire? In your imagination envision Christ in the synagogue looking you in the face and asking, "What is it you seek? What do you want?"

5   For at least ten minutes go back over the whole of the gospel passage, allowing the story to unfold further in your imagination. Who is there? What is being said? What is being done?

6   Gather together the main strands of your contemplation. Spend a few minutes giving attention to the parts of the contemplation that most deeply moved you. Conclude by saying the Lord's Prayer.

3

Contemplative Awareness

*Now more than ever the word about Jesus spread abroad;
many crowds would gather to hear him and to be cured of
their diseases. But he would withdraw to deserted places
and pray. (Lk 5:15-16)*

Words from the Book of Psalms, "Be still and know that I am God" (Ps 46:10), point to the heart of the practice of prayer. They also suggest what it was that Jesus was doing when he withdrew "to deserted places," as St. Luke says. He would go out to the mountain to pray (Lk 6:12), or would get up early in the morning while it was still very dark (Mk 1:35). The picture portrayed is that of regular moments of stillness.

Sometimes it is assumed that prayer is entirely about uttering words. In part it is that. At a deeper level, however, prayer is about being still and aware at an inner level of the One who is closer to us than we are to ourselves. It is a silent attentiveness to the Life that is at the heart of all life. Prayer is a listening to the Word that was in the beginning and through which we and all created things have been "uttered" into being.

An old woman of prayer once told me that for years whenever she had knelt to pray she would begin to yawn. It was because she had thought that prayer consisted mainly of what *she* had to say, and what *she* had to say was pretty much the same day after day. She now realized that prayer was primarily about listening for God and, only after listening at levels deeper than word and thought, responding. Of course she had yawned! Prayer had become for her a monologue in which she repeated herself again and again. Now, however, she saw that it was a time to *listen.* She became alert in prayer, attentive to God's Spirit within her spirit, stirring her to new awakenings.

Jesus speaks in one of his gospel parables of servants who had their lamps lit, waiting attentively for the coming of their master. The unexpected twist of the story is that when they open the door it is the *master* who serves *them* (Lk 12:35ff). A parable will have many meanings, but in part this story points to the need for an inner watchfulness, so that when doors of God open within us we are indeed alert. Prayer is a time of being reawakened in our hearts, restored in the depths of who we are. It is being fed on the fare of God's life within us, an awareness of our heart being touched by God's heart.

To be attentively still in any context of life is to be more aware, whether that be of our body and breathing, or of sounds and color and light around us. In prayer we enter an *inner* stillness, for "the kingdom of God," says Jesus, "is within you" (Lk 17:21). Prayer is an attentiveness to this paradise of God within, and not only within *us* but within *all life*. It is invisible, like yeast mixed into flour, a hidden presence, says Jesus, but one that leavens the whole (Lk 13:21). It is the mystery of the Life that is at the heart of life.

The reality for most of us much of the time is that we live in a type of exile from that paradise. As Henri Nouwen said, "We have a home address, but we aren't often there." We live at a distance from our true home. Like clay off-center on a potter's wheel, our lives and relationships become wobbly and distorted. Prayer is a return to the center, or to what T. S. Eliot calls "the still point of the turning world." There we regain awareness of where our life and all life is rooted. There we uncover again what is so easily buried in the confusions of daily life—our grounding in God. It is easy to persuade ourselves that we are too busy to pray, or that our activities are so all-important that we cannot afford the regular times of stillness that will open doors within us to such awareness and remembering. But Jesus says, "Seek first God's kingdom" (Lk

12:31). Prayer is a refocusing of our lives. It prepares us to live out of the paradise that is at the beginning and center of life.

In the gospel story of the prodigal, the younger son goes out in search of fulfilment but his quest for satisfaction becomes self-destructive. In telling the story, Jesus says that when "he came to himself" the prodigal realized what he should do (Lk 15:17). Similarly, prayer is about being reminded of who we are, namely sons and daughters of God. It is a return to ourselves. In prayer we are being re-collected to the center of life rather than being pulled this way and that on the surface of life's busyness to find our fulfilment and identity. Jesus goes off to the desert to pray. Even, and maybe especially, when his popularity is high, he seeks a recentering.

In the third century, St. Antony of Egypt, the first of the "Desert Fathers," used to say to his followers: "When you die and stand before God in judgment, you will not be asked whether you have become another Antony, or Paul, or even the great Mary herself, but whether you have become truly yourself." The traditional emphasis on repentance during the season of Lent is not that we should become something other than ourselves, but rather that we should become truly ourselves. The gospel is given not to tell us that we have failed, for we more or less know that about ourselves. Rather the gospel is given to make known to us what we have forgotten, and that is who we are. The goodness of God's image is planted deep within us. The discipline of contemplative prayer is about listening to that truth and being set free by it.

Where are our places of stillness, and *when* are they? They do not have to be explicitly religious. Time in a side chapel, or moments of silence somewhere in prayer, may open inner doors of awareness in us. But so may minutes in a garden, or times of quiet by a window or in a chosen room in the house. We will know within ourselves when we have experienced contemplative stillness. We will also know whether we should be seeking such moments more often.

On the island of Patmos in the Aegean, I met a man who had very little to do with the church. Yet it was his custom after work each day to enter a little chapel on his family property – the type of small white-washed shrine that dots the Greek landscape in so many places, in order to be still. When I asked him what he did during that time of silence, he answered, "Nothing, I simply sit." And when I asked why, he said, "Because my father, and before him my father's father, spent time here in silence every day." At a level deeper than formal belief, this man knew within himself the reality of being renewed through a daily practice of silence.

This is not to say that the practice of contemplative prayer is an easy one. Being still before God may have a beautiful simplicity about it, but in fact it can be difficult to find and sustain. Distractions crowd into our minds and drive us in all sorts of directions. Nor is it to imply that the awarenesses that arise in us in prayer are always easy to live with or to be true to. If our desire has been to learn from Jesus' practice and to seek our own "deserted place" of prayer, the result will often be a realization that we did not really know what it was we were asking for. Fears and anxieties can arise out of the silence, as can disturbing and challenging truths. Prayer is no hideaway! It is not just about our own space being protected for a while in order that we be renewed. This is not to underestimate the importance of time alone, the need for which varies between different people and at different stages in life. Rather it is to say that contemplative silence is not simply to be equated with time away from others.

Jesus says, "If any want to become my followers, let them deny themselves and take up their cross daily and follow me" (Lk 9:23). This applies as much, and perhaps even more, to the practice of prayer as it does to any other aspect of following Christ. The paradise of God is deep within us, and contemplative prayer is an experienced awareness of that truth in the heart of our being. But in prayer there is also the need to "die to self" if we are to uncover the treasure within, to become aware of the falseness in us that obscures that truth. An awareness in prayer of what is untrue in us, and the choosing to die to these things, is what will then undergird our decisions to be self-giving in our lives. Prayer is about "being undone" in the things that are not rooted in the Self of God within us. We are challenged to die to everything that obscures the image of love at the heart of who we are. Far from being a hideaway, prayer is a place where we are stripped down.

The place called "The White Strand of the Monks" on Iona is a beautiful stretch of beach at the north end of the island. It has been a place of sanctuary over the centuries for countless numbers of men and women searching for solitude and stillness. And yet this place of such exquisite beauty, where earth, sea and sky seem to open out into the eternal, has also been a site of terrible pain and dismemberment. Here in the ninth century the monks on Iona, confident in "that which cannot be seen," as the writer to the Hebrews says (Heb 11:1), faced martyrdom at the hands of Norse invaders. Red blood was spilt on the pure white sands.

Thus while prayer is a movement within our hearts toward what is truest and most beautiful, it is also marked by moments of costly passage. This in part is why the desert has traditionally been a place of prayer, and why in Lent we especially remember Jesus' forty days in the wilderness (Lk 4:1–13). Its vast emptiness outwardly reflects the inner reality of being stripped down to our essence. It is only in such unencumbered nakedness that we are free to move closer to the heart of life, divested of everything that cuts us off from the place of God within. As Jesus says to the penitent thief on the cross, who is about to lose everything, "Today you will be with me in Paradise" (Lk 23:43). It is in dying to the outward and to everything that is false in us that we will find our true selves, rooted in God.

The promise of the gospel is that, deeper than being undone, deeper even than death, is life. If in the "deserted place" of prayer we allow ourselves to be stripped before God, then our true selves, bearing the creative and untameable mystery of God's image, will more and more be reborn in us. It is God's "good pleasure," says Jesus, to lead us into that paradise (Lk 12:33). Let us turn our hearts to what he calls "the unfailing treasure," the place "where no thief comes near and no moth can destroy."

Gospel Contemplation

1   Prepare for the gospel contemplation by being still for a few minutes. Be aware of God's presence within and all around you.

2   Read and reread the gospel passage (Lk 5:15-16), letting its details settle in your memory.

3   Imagine the deserted place to which Jesus withdraws to pray. What is it like? Spend at least five minutes using the senses of your imagination to see, hear, smell, taste and touch the place. Allow it to be a combination of places that you have known in your life.

4   What is your heart's desire? In your imagination envision Christ in the deserted place looking you in the face and asking, "What is it you seek? What do you want?"

5   For at least ten minutes go back over the whole of the gospel passage, allowing the story to unfold further in your imagination. Who is there? What is being said? What is being done?

6   Gather together the main strands of your contemplation. Spend a few minutes giving attention to the parts of the contemplation that most deeply moved you. Conclude by saying the Lord's Prayer.

4

Prayer as Heart's Desire

Jesus came out and went, as was his custom, to the Mount of Olives; and the disciples followed him. When he reached the place, he said to them, "Pray that you may not come into temptation." Then he withdrew from them about a stone's throw, knelt down, and prayed, "Father, if you are willing, remove this cup from me; yet, not my will but yours be done." Then an angel from heaven appeared to him and gave him strength. In his anguish he prayed more earnestly, and his sweat became like great drops of blood falling down on the ground. When he got up from prayer, he came to the disciples and found them sleeping because of grief, and he said to them, "Why are you sleeping? Get up and pray that you may not come into temptation." (Lk 22:39-46)

I t is to a garden that Jesus goes to pray. Here he faces the anguish that is within him as he approaches his time of suffering. In prayer he is searching in the inner garden of his soul for a strength that is greater than the fear that shakes his body. The garden is not a place of escape, nor is prayer. It is not an attempt to deny or hide from the powers of death that threaten him. Rather it is a way of confronting them and recognizing the sorrow and fear that are in his soul. In the face of these he expresses his yearnings for life. He prays, "remove this cup from me."

To the disciples he says, "Pray that you may not come into temptation." And he says it again, "Pray that you may not come into temptation." What does he mean? Is he not pointing to a temptation in them to flee the place of suffering, and to betray their love of him? In part he is warning them not to be false to themselves, and guiding them as to where they can find the strength to be true. His words can be paraphrased, "Pray that you may be true to yourselves."

To follow temptation is to live out of the fears and confusions that obscure what we most truly are, namely, made in God's image. It is about being false, for instance, to the passion for love and faithfulness that is planted at the heart of who we are. The key to prayer is truthfulness to our hearts. Without this we will not move far into the inner garden of our souls. We will neither be aware of its infinite depths, nor be able to give expression to the desires that surge up from far beneath our understanding.

To remain at the surface of life is to be out of touch with what lies within us. We consist of so much more than the exterior of our lives. Why then do we so often ignore the depths of who we are? Is it because, like the disciples in our gospel story, we have fallen asleep? Outwardly we may appear to be awake, but the reality is that in many dimensions of life we are sleepwalking. We can be totally unaware of some of the things that are coursing through us like subterranean streams. Again and again we choose to deny fears and uncertainties that inwardly may be tearing us apart. The disciples, says St. Luke, slept "because of grief." They could not bear to face the suffering of the one they loved.

What is it in our depths that we are called to be true to in prayer? In the first instance it is our heart's desires. The deepest yearnings in us issue up from the image of God in which we have been made. Our desires for life and well-being, for new beginnings and creativity, and most of all for faithfulness and love have their source in the life of God at the heart of our lives. Yes, of course there are other desires in us as well. We know the selfish and destructive passions that can suddenly overwhelm us. They will sometimes have a dementing power of disorientation over us. But do we know that deeper than these are the passionate desires for life and wholeness that God has planted at the heart of our being?

Jesus' teachings about prayer, and more importantly his practice of prayer, show how important it is to utter our heart's desires. "Give us our daily bread" (Lk 11:3), "forgive us our sins" (Lk 11:4), "rescue us from evil" (Lk 11:4) are expressions from the heart of life. If we do not experience them as such then we need to ask if we are in fact living at a distance from our deepest desires and from the hearts of men and women throughout the world, many of whom are desperately yearning for food for their families, or new beginnings out of failure, or release from terrible wrongs. Jesus says, "ask... seek...knock" (Lk 11:9). Be persistent like the widow who would not let go of her passion for justice (Lk 18:1ff). Remain in touch with the desires of your heart that arise from within you. Cry out with them day and night, he says (Lk 18:7).

The theme of repentance in Lent is a call to return to what is deepest in us. The essence of repentance is not about turning away *from* ourselves but about returning *to* ourselves. To turn around is to leave what is false in us in order to be led by Christ to the goodness and beauty that lie at the center of who we are. One of the angelic pronouncements concerning the prophet John the Baptist is that he will "turn the hearts of parents to their children" (Lk 1:17). What is more natural for parents than to love their children? And yet so often we live contrary to that love. Our hearts become withdrawn, even from those with whom we are most naturally connected. The grace of repentance frees us to recover the goodness of the desires that have been naturally planted by God in the depths of our hearts.

The *true* place of prayer, then, is never an escape from life and from the struggles of the world. It is about moving into a deeper consciousness of them and allowing our hearts to be touched by them. Whether in a remote desert space of stillness, or in the midst of the busyness of life, prayer is not about *stepping away* from the world, but about *approaching its center*. In such prayer we will be alive to the fears as well as the hopes that are in us. This in turn will awaken us to the fears and hopes that are in others too. Our hearts can then be touched by their brokenness of heart, and our yearnings by their yearnings.

In St. Luke's Gospel, many of the healing stories are marked by a sense of Jesus' compassion being touched by the passion of others. In Nain, it is the sight of a woman weeping by the side of her dead son. "He was his mother's only son," writes Luke, "and she was a widow" (Lk 7:12). Which one of us does not know something of the unbearableness of that sort of pain, even if it is just the fear of such loss? And perhaps even more poignant are the desperate words of a father speaking of the horror of his son's confusions and suffering. His direct plea to Jesus is, "He is my only son" (Lk 9:38). When we allow ourselves to be in touch, either with the pain that is in us or the anguish that we hear in another's soul, our cry of the heart is, "Remove this cup of suffering. Take away this sorrow."

When Jesus so prays in the garden a grace of God is given him in the form of an angel of strength. The strength that he receives, however, is not one that lifts him out of the struggle that he is experiencing. Rather it takes him further into it. "In his anguish he prayed more earnestly," writes Luke, "and his sweat became like great drops of blood falling down on the ground." So it is for us in our times of weakness when we seek God's strength. The messengers who bring us the grace of strength are always bearers of love as well, and the gift of love moves us to confront what threatens life, not to run away from it. Have we not known this in our lives when a person whom we love has enabled us to be true to ourselves and to what we hold dear? The presence of such a person does not draw us out of the reality of struggle in life, but rather fortifies us for that struggle.

Let us be quite clear that the Christian mystery is *not* about being airlifted out of suffering. The cup of suffering is not removed from Jesus. The expression of his heart's desire does not free him from the agony that is to come. His words, "remove this cup from me," reflect his passion for life and the pain that he experiences at the prospect of losing life and being torn from those he loves. His prayer is an expression of the love that is in him, and he is strengthened in that love so as to be led further into the way of God. It is a way that leads to gaining life by losing it.

Great people of prayer often bear visibly in their faces something of the suffering of the world. They convey from within themselves a sense of the beauty that is at the heart of life. They know also, however, that it is a beauty shrouded in pain. The journey to God, and into the beauty at the heart of life, is *through* pain, not *around* it. To be opened by love is to become vulnerable both to the beauty and to the suffering. Do we not all know this to be true? When we have had to witness with a sense of powerlessness the suffering of another, whether that be our child or friend or lover, have we not at such moments known that love draws us into the agony and not away from it?

To live in that tension as Jesus did in the garden is to express our passion for life, and also to bow to the deeper mystery that unfolds itself through a dying to ourselves. It is to know the intermingling of the grace of living and the grace of dying, the desire to experience life's goodness, and at the same time to know that to let go is to be led more deeply into life. And so Jesus prays in the garden, "remove this cup from me; yet, not my will but yours be done."

Gospel Contemplation

1 Prepare for the gospel contemplation by being still for a few minutes. Be aware of God's presence within and all around you.

2 Read and reread the gospel passage (Lk 22:39–46), letting its details settle in your memory.

3 Imagine the garden in which Jesus is praying. What is it like? Spend at least five minutes using the senses of your imagination to see, hear, smell, taste and touch the place. Allow it to be a combination of places that you have known in your life.

4 What is your heart's desire? In your imagination envision Christ in the garden looking you in the face and asking, "What is it you seek? What do you want?"

5 For at least ten minutes go back over the whole of the gospel passage, allowing the story to unfold further in your imagination. Who is there? What is being said? What is being done?

6 Gather together the main strands of your contemplation. Spend a few minutes giving attention to the parts of the contemplation that most deeply moved you. Conclude by saying the Lord's Prayer.

5

Sharing the Brokenness

One of the Pharisees asked Jesus to eat with him, and he went into the Pharisee's house and took his place at the table. And a woman in the city, who was a sinner, having learned that he was eating in the Pharisee's house, brought an alabaster jar of ointment. She stood behind him at his feet, weeping, and began to bathe his feet with her tears and to dry them with her hair. Then she continued kissing his feet and anointing them with the ointment. Now when the Pharisee who had invited him saw it, he said to himself, "If this man were a prophet, he would have known who and what kind of woman this is who is touching him—that she is a sinner." Jesus spoke up and said to him, "Simon, I have something to say to you."...Then turning toward the woman, he said to Simon, "Do you see this woman? I entered your house; you gave me no water for my feet, but she has bathed my feet with her tears and dried them with her hair. You gave me no kiss, but from the time I came in she has not stopped kissing my feet. You did not anoint my head with oil, but she has anointed my feet with ointment. Therefore, I tell you, her sins, which were many, have been forgiven; hence she has shown great love. But the one to whom little is forgiven, loves little." (Lk 7:36-47)

esus allows a woman of the city "who was a sinner," says Luke, to touch him. This was contrary to respectable practice. She was an "untouchable." It upset his host, a strict observer of religious law. Repeatedly Jesus was criticized for identifying with those outside the bounds of propriety. Again and again the religious leaders of the day complained about him eating with "tax collectors and sinners" (Lk 5:30, 7:34, 15:2, 19:7). Consequently, he himself came to be described as "a glutton and a drunkard" (Lk 7:32).

The terms *tax collector* and *sinner* refer to those who for different reasons were rejected by the religion of the day. Tax collectors were despised because they collaborated with the foreign occupation of Judea. They did the dirty work of the Roman Empire, collecting revenue from their own oppressed people and taking a cut for themselves. Sinners referred to those outside the bounds of religious practice, uneducated in its laws and traditions. Jesus identifies himself with these, and he does so by going as far as sharing food with them, which in his day was a mark of the closest of identifications.

By being with those outside religion in this way, Jesus does not, however, provide a neat blueprint for our engagement with the world today. We are *not* told exactly what to say or do. But we *are* given a clear picture of the way in which he engaged with people. In this gospel story the rejected woman senses that she is accepted by Jesus, long before he utters these words of forgiveness. By being with her and allowing her to come close, he communicates a generosity of spirit that is deeper than words and religious expression. That is why "she has shown great love," he says. Her repentance is a response to his forgiving spirit, not a prerequisite to it.

Jesus' practice emphasizes the common ground that is

between the religious and the non-religious, or between the Church and the world. St. Luke's way of putting it, in his genealogy of Jesus, is to describe him as "son of Adam, son of God" (Lk 3:38). This is to say that as all are of Adam's life, so all are of God's. It is to see every man and woman bearing the holy image, born in essence of God.

To find the common ground between us is to move deeper than what distinguishes us from each other. It can allow us to live out of the unity that underlies life, instead of out of the differences that characterize it at its surface. The list of differences is of course endless, whether between male and female, rich and poor, black and white, homosexual and heterosexual, or between Christian and non-Christian. This is not to deny the differences, nor the pain of separation and conflict that can arise from them. Rather it is to ask, "What is the way forward, beyond division?" Is it not, in part, to return again and again to the common ground that we share, and to build from that foundation?

To begin to know the unity that we share with all people, each one made in the image of God, is not primarily to name the ways in which we differ, or have each fallen from that image. Much more important is to be able to name and redeem in one another the goodness of God's life. In our gospel story, Jesus affirms the presence of the woman. He does not play up her failure, but releases what is best and truest in her, her tears and her love.

What are the truest dimensions of one another that we can be part of redeeming? Will it not be to do with what is deepest in our hearts, with the affection we feel for our children, with the creative and passionate energies in us that may have been locked away, with our desires for love and new beginnings in life, and yearnings for peace and well-being? To engage with the best that is in others, whether that be in the church or in the world, is not first to accentuate our differences but to point to the rich common stream of God's life flowing within all life. It is to find ways of celebrating what at some level we all know to be true—the sacred mystery of every newborn child and of the rising sun each day. How shall we communicate our sense of the shared holiness of life before enunciating the distinctiveness of our beliefs? Only in the context of what we share should we speak of why we baptize our children, for instance, or why we believe in God as the Light within the morning light.

Not only does Jesus walk in the common ground but he is willing to point to a greatness of spirit when he sees it in those outside religious acceptability. Like Simon the Pharisee in our gospel story, we perhaps have been the ones to throw a party for Jesus, providing good food and wine. We may even have done so out of a love for him, and a desire to introduce him to our friends. But have we also shared our struggles and tears, like the unwanted woman? Have *we* been prepared to show that we are broken people?

In another story, the parable of the tax collector and the Pharisee (Lk 18:9ff), Jesus describes the latter as saying, "God, I thank you that I am not like other people: thieves, rogues, adulterers, or even like this tax collector." The tax collector, on the other hand, whose sense of unworthiness does not even allow him to lift his eyes in prayer, cries out, "God, be merciful to me, a sinner!" Most of us will have met people of such humility outside the bounds of religion. It is to such as these that Jesus points when he speaks of a beauty or beatitude of spirit. "All who exalt themselves will be humbled," says Jesus, "but all who humble themselves will be exalted" (Lk 18:14). Not only are we to live out of a sense of the glory and the brokenness that are within all people; we are also to know that it will often be in people outside our religious boundaries that we see the clearest reflections of God's beauty of spirit.

What was it about the woman bathing Jesus' feet with her tears that so annoyed Simon? Was it that, just by being there, she stirred within him an awareness of his own failings and his own need for repentance? Simon can represent the tendency to show only what is "nice" and respectable in our religious selves, what is ordered and pleasant. We know, of course, that there is much more down in the basement of who we are. There are shadows overlapping the light. There is memory of past failure, and awareness of present confusion and temptation. At one level there can be no doubt in us that we share the world's brokenness in the failures and struggles of our lives. But how successful have we been at translating that into a humility of relationship with the world? Have we not preferred, if we can get away with it, to give the impression that we are in a different category? The reality is that in the end we do not often fool others, nor can we at heart really fool ourselves. In our life of engagement with the world, we need to be candid about the false self that is as unsettling in us as it is in anyone else.

A good woman of the church once told me of the important things she was doing in the wider community. She confessed, however, to not being able to have people into her house because it was such a mess. At various levels this is exactly what can happen in our relationship with the world. We want to hide away the messes of our lives, even though in one way or another they usually seep out. This is not to say that every detail of every struggle needs to be known by everyone. It is, rather, to point to the need for an authenticity of relationship. It is to engage on the basis of knowing that we carry within ourselves the types of brokenness that we witness in the world.

Jesus criticizes the Pharisees for their excessive concern about outward appearance. You clean only "the outside of the cup," he says. "Did not the one who made the outside make the inside also?" (Lk 19:39ff). He speaks of the need above all else to offer what is within ourselves. Our engagement with the world is part of our engagement with God, for God is the Life of the world. In prayer we allow our hearts to be touched by the hearts of suffering men and women. Similarly, in relationship with the world our hearts are to be open so that we may be touched. That will include showing something of the brokenness that is in us. We need to confess that our journey is not one of only peace and certainty. The confusions and doubts that belong to all humanity belong to us.

Why is it that we so often find it difficult to be transparent about the failures and brokenness of our lives? Have we lost touch with the deeper truth of who we are, made in God's image, and the unshakeable inner security that can come with that knowledge? In our engagement with the world, let us be set free by the truth, not to deny that there is failure and brokenness in us, but to proclaim that deeper still is the life of God. At the heart of our lives is the redemptive desire of God to restore us. Forgiveness is the grace that awakens us to that holy yearning. To know that we have failed, and to know that in our failure the Lover still desires us, is to be opened further to love. The depth of that experience, indicates Jesus, will be the depth of our loving.

Gospel Contemplation

1   Prepare for the gospel contemplation by being still for a few minutes. Be aware of God's presence within and all around you.

2   Read and reread the gospel passage (Lk 7:36–47), letting its details settle in your memory.

3   Imagine the house in which Jesus is eating. What is it like? Spend at least five minutes using the senses of your imagination to see, hear, smell, taste and touch the place. Allow it to be a combination of places that you have known in your life.

4   What is your heart's desire? In your imagination envision Christ at the table looking you in the face and asking, "What is it you seek? What do you want?"

5   For at least ten minutes go back over the whole of the gospel passage, allowing the story to unfold further in your imagination. Who is there? What is being said? What is being done?

6   Gather together the main strands of your contemplation. Spend a few minutes giving attention to the parts of the contemplation that most deeply moved you. Conclude by saying the Lord's Prayer.

6

Passion for Change

As Jesus was now approaching the path down from the Mount of Olives, the whole multitude of the disciples began to praise God joyfully with a loud voice for all the deeds of power that they had seen, saying, "Blessed is the king who comes in the name of the Lord! Peace in heaven, and glory in the highest heaven!" Some of the Pharisees in the crowd said to him, "Teacher, order your disciples to stop." He answered, "I tell you, if these were silent, the stones would shout out." As he came near and saw the city, he wept over it, saying, "If you, even you, had only recognized on this day the things that make for peace! But now they are hidden from your eyes." (Lk 19:37-42)

I s there anything of value in life, whether physical or spiritual, that happens without passion, passion for creativity and expression, passion for knowing and loving? Life is conceived and born out of passion, and it is passion that can redeem and transform our lives when they are overshadowed by the things of death.

Jesus approaches Jerusalem. He gazes over the city that he loves, and he is angry in the nation's holy place. His reaction is fired by passion, as is his death, only days later, in the place called "The Skull." The uninhibited song of the crowd that accompanies his entry into Jerusalem, his weeping over the city, and his fury in the Temple are all passionate expressions of life and love.

"As he was now approaching the path down from the Mount of Olives," says St. Luke, "the whole multitude of the disciples began to praise God joyfully with a loud voice." As much as this description can begin to sound like gospel-hall singing, it points primarily to a letting go. True praise issues out of the very soul of who we are, in our bodies, minds and spirits. It is about holding nothing back in offering ourselves to God in love, including our deepest physical and spiritual energies.

My memory of singing and dancing to drum beat in the cloister of Iona Abbey around a sensuously shaped statue of Mary, originally called "Our Lady of Delight," is one of some embarrassment. I am not just speaking about how others responded, but of the inhibition or holding back that I experienced in myself. Worship in the western tradition rarely moves deeper than the neck, and if it touches the emotions it is often criticized as "charismatic." Some of our deepest physical energies are often presumed to be absent during worship. This is not to pretend that our natural energies, including the sexual, are not also terribly confused and misdirected at times. It is rather to say that their confusion will often result from not having been addressed as part of our spirituality.

True praise draws on what has been most deeply planted in us. This is to hold together the mysteries of creation and redemption. The God who redeems us is the God who created us. Redemption is about being restored to our most truly natural selves. To worship God, therefore, with our souls and bodies, as our post-communion prayer says, is to offer to God the goodness of our spiritual and physical senses. It is to be further awakened in the fullness of who we are to a more passionate engagement with the One who is at the heart of life.

Jesus responds to those who are critical of the uninhibited song of the disciples by saying, "if these were silent, the stones would shout out." His reference to the stones points to the mystery of relationship between God and creation, and the song of praise that creation sings. "There is no speech, nor are there words," says the Psalmist—referring to the song of the sun, moon and stars—"yet their voice goes out through all the earth" (Ps 19:3-4). The explosive song of the expanding universe is a hymn that goes on whether we join it or not. As an Irish priest friend of mine used to say, "If from the beginning of time to today is like a 24-hour clock, then the arrival of humanity on that clock is one minute before midnight." We are latecomers indeed! Our voice is part of, and needs to be guided by, the ongoing hymn of the universe. It is a wild and uncontained song that is sung every morning in the fire of the rising sun, and in the dark fecundity of the growing earth. To be stirred passionately to praise is to be awakened at depths within ourselves to the sacredness of all life. It kindles in us a deeper desire to be engaged with the life of world.

In approaching Jerusalem, Jesus' heart was alert to the city he loved. The sight of it would have evoked in him memories from his own life and the history of his people. To view it, and at the same time know that it had become a city cut off from its spiritual foundations, was to see it collapsing. His words, "If you...had only recognized the things that make for peace," speak of a city that has missed its moment. They give the impression of a people caught in a self-chosen spiral of destruction. When Jesus sees the city, he weeps. Later, in St. Luke's passion narrative, he encourages the "Daughters of Jerusalem" to do the same. "Weep for yourselves," he says, "and for your children" (Lk 23:28).

What are the places in our lives, the villages or open countryside, the islands or cities, that evoke in us a deep response? If we witness the desecration of places that hold such depth of memory and affection for us, or see them departing from the goodness and beauty that we have known to be in them, what is the passion that stirs in us? On a larger scale we can think of cities and countries throughout the world that are being ripped apart by hatreds that seem intractable, or by degradations of spirit and obsessive pursuits that inflict a type of self-ruin. What are we to do? Jesus enters the city.

Jesus' practice *does not* provide us with a blueprint of exactly what we are to say or do. It *does,* however, point to the need to allow our hearts to be pierced by the sorrow of what we witness in the world, and then to live in relation to that sorrow. We are not all called literally to enter the city. But we are called to allow the core of who we are to be touched by the brokenness of such places. We are not to wait until we know exactly what to say or do in the face of an injustice or wrong. Such uncertainty can paralyze us into doing nothing. Our first commitment is to keep our hearts open. This will ensure that the passion in us for change will not die.

As we search for what it is we are to say or do in any particular situation, let us above all else be aware that the creative Word resides within us. We are to speak it out of our very being, at levels deeper than what can be outwardly heard. We can be bearers of it in the places we love by simply choosing to be there. Whether in silence, or in times of audibly speaking and acting for justice, the passion of God can be uttered in our lives.

When he chooses to be in the city that is heading towards self-destruction, Jesus' passion moves from sorrow to anger as he enters the temple. What should have been the heart of the city's wisdom, the place where a knowledge of what makes for true peace could be fostered, has become instead "a den of robbers," as he says (Lk 19:46). Instead of guiding the people of the city towards well-being, it only mirrors the wrongs of the city. Jesus had insisted that the poor, the crippled, the lame and the blind were to be favored (Lk 14:13). Instead, what he finds in the temple is a system of money-exchange and the sale of sacrificial offerings that is either exploiting or denying the devotion of these very people. With a passion like that expressed in the words of the Magnificat, "showing strength with his arm," "scattering the proud," "bringing down the powerful," and "lifting up the lowly" (Lk 1:51–52), Jesus cleanses the temple.

It is Jesus' passionate words and actions that all along had frightened the establishment. He *wept* at the sight of the city; the religious leaders shed no tears. His entry into

Jerusalem was accompanied by *unrestrained* songs of praise; they urged him to stop the singing. He *angrily* swept the temple of abuse; they were prepared to benefit from the profiteering. Moreover, the Pharisees and priests were the very ones who could have strengthened the city's foundations for peace. Instead they were, in fact, shaking its cornerstone. Jesus directs his passionate anger at them. "Woe to you Pharisees!" says Jesus. "For you tithe mint and rue and herbs of all kinds, and neglect justice and the love of God. ...Woe to you lawyers! For you have taken away the key of knowledge; you did not enter yourselves, and you hindered those who were entering" (Lk 11:42–52).

We need to ask if we are passionate about what makes for peace in our cities, communities and nations. We find it easier to analyze intellectually the sorts of things that must be done to build peace. There is considerable agreement on such matters. The challenge is whether we are prepared to descend from the moral high ground into "the city," into the places of confusion and violence in order to be bearers of peace. Jesus' way, as St. Paul says, was "making peace by the blood of his cross" (Col 1:20). It is a costly way. The movement is from passionate *longing* towards passionate *self-giving*.

It is the passion of self-giving, the giving of our hearts and time and creativity, that will make for peace in our relationships and world. Although the truth of following this passion may be hidden from our eyes, as Jesus says, it is not far from us. God's wisdom, as Sirach says, was created with us "in the womb" (Sir 1:14). It is at the heart of who we are. Promptings from this place of wisdom are what will guide us in the journey towards peace. The springs of God's passion are deep within us.

Gospel Contemplation

1 Prepare for the gospel contemplation by being still for a few minutes. Be aware of God's presence within and all around you.

2 Read and reread the gospel passage (Lk 19:37–42), letting its details settle in your memory.

3 Imagine the path into the city on which Jesus is walking. What is it like? Spend at least five minutes using the senses of your imagination to see, hear, smell, taste and touch the place. Allow it to be a combination of places that you have known in your life.

4 What is your heart's desire? In your imagination envision Christ on the road to Jerusalem looking you in the face and asking, "What is it you seek? What do you want?"

5 For at least ten minutes go back over the whole of the gospel passage, allowing the story to unfold further in your imagination. Who is there? What is being said? What is being done?

6 Gather together the main strands of your contemplation. Spend a few minutes giving attention to the parts of the contemplation that most deeply moved you. Conclude by saying the Lord's Prayer.

Appendix

A Guide for Group Use

If the gospel contemplations are used in a group context, it is important that there be a simple structure that will facilitate confidence about being silent together as well as sharing as a group. The following notes are for a group facilitator.

Introduction

◆ Make sure the venue, whether a side chapel or a room in a house, is appropriate for the size as well as the nature of the gathering. Because there will be a full 30 minutes of silence, it is important that the setting not be too crowded, for instance, or too cold.

◆ It can be helpful to mark the beginning of the group's time together by lighting a candle, for example, or listening to a piece of music.

◆ People should have read in advance the chapter for the week, but *briefly* introduce the week's theme with reference to the gospel passage.

◆ Remind them of the overall shape of the meeting, i.e. gospel contemplation, small-group reflection, and large-group sharing. The intention is not to discuss the content of the relevant chapter but to share an experience of contemplation together.

Gospel Contemplation

- Point the group to the gospel contemplation notes at the end of the relevant chapter.
- Read aloud twice the gospel passage.
- Allow 30 minutes of silence for the contemplation exercise.
- Finish the contemplation by saying together the Lord's prayer:

Our Father in heaven,

hallowed be your name,

your kingdom come,

your will be done,

on earth as in heaven.

Give us today our daily bread.

Forgive us our sins

as we forgive those who sin against us.

Lead us not into temptation

but deliver us from evil.

For the kingdom, the power,

and the glory are yours

now and forever.

Amen.

Small-group Reflection

◆ Instruct people to turn to their neighbor(s) and, in groups of two or three, share anything they wish to from their gospel contemplation.

◆ Allow 15 minutes for this.

Large-group Sharing

◆ Call people back into the large group and invite them to share from their individual contemplations. This is a time for listening to one another, not for commenting on one another's experiences or reflections.

◆ If everyone in turn is to be given time to share, it is important to make it very clear that sharing aloud is not mandatory. Some will prefer to be silent. It can be help-ful in such cases to provide everyone with a symbol, a stone for example, that can be placed in silence beside a candle or a cross in the center of the group as a sign of giving thanks for the contemplation, without having to talk about it.

◆ Allow 30 minutes for this.

◆ Close the discussion by saying together:

The grace of our Lord Jesus Christ,

the love of God,

and the fellowship of the Holy Spirit,

be with us all ever more.

Amen.